More Than Overcomers

Devotions for the Lenten Season

Lynne Modranski

Mansion Hill Press

More Than Overcomers
Devotions for the Lenten Season
by Lynne Modranski

© 2021 Lynne Modranski

Published by Mansion Hill Press
Steubenville, OH 43952

Print ISBN: 978-1-953374-04-2
E-Book/EPUB ISBN: 978-1-953374-05-9
LCCN: 2021902152

All rights reserved. No portion may be reproduced digitally or physically without written consent of the author except for excerpts quoted in reviews or inspirational documents.

Scripture taken or paraphrased from:

Holy Bible, New International Version®, NIV® Copyright ©1973, 1978, 1984, 2011 by Biblica, Inc.® Used by permission. All rights reserved worldwide.

Holman Christian Standard Bible®, Copyright © 1999, 2000, 2002, 2003, 2009 by Holman Bible Publishers. Used by permission. Holman Christian Standard Bible®, Holman CSB®, and HCSB® are federally registered trademarks of Holman Bible Publishers.

OTHER BOOKS BY LYNNE MODRANSKI

Dive In to a Life of Freedom
Devotions for Church Leaders and Small Group
Devotions Inspired by Life
Quiet Times for Busy Moms
A Reflection of the Beauty of God

A Note to You

Welcome to Lent. The season begins six and a half weeks before Easter on a day we've come to call Ash Wednesday. Christians set aside this time as holy during the time of the apostles, and in 325 A.D. the church council made it official.

You'll find all kinds of rules and traditions associated with these weeks, but the season's main purpose is to bring us closer to Jesus.

I pray you'll add some spiritual discipline to your daily routine, hopefully by the end of six weeks it will be so integral you'll continue long after Easter has passed. Richard Foster gives us twelve areas of discipline to get started. He includes:

- Meditation (for instance focusing on scripture and devotions like you'll find in this book)
- Prayer
- Fasting
- Study
- Simplicity
- Solitude
- Submission
- Service
- Confession
- Worship
- Guidance
- Celebration

Don't attempt to add them all at one time. If you choose one to focus on every other month, you'll have added them all in just two years. And even if you only add one a year, you're growing. That's all that matters.

May the short devotions that follow bring you many aha moments and help you dive deeper into a relationship with your Savior!

Living Blessed,

Lynne

Ash Wednesday

There is, therefore, now no condemnation for those who are in Christ Jesus
Romans 8:1

No condemnation. No blame. No criticism. No disapproval. No reprimand. No sentence. No judgement. No punishment. No whistle blowing. No finding fault or pointing fingers for those who are in Christ Jesus.

Perhaps this explains why I'm so attracted to Romans 8. As a perfectionist, second guessing myself has become almost a hobby, and not necessarily a fun hobby. I judge myself more often than I judge others. Romans 8 lets me off the hook. I decided only arrogance would condemn someone Jesus declared not guilty.

Six weeks prior to Easter, we begin a season called Lent, a season of retrospect and self-examination. Many use these weeks for fasting, and the period offers an opportunity for repentance. It's good to take a break from life to sit in the balance and make sure we're living up to Christ's sacrifice on the cross.

Regrettably, retrospect and self-examination can tempt us to condemn. The enemy will use the opportunity to whisper words of shame. And instead of listening to Christ's Spirit encouraging us to become all He created us to be, we end up magnifying the misdeed rather than the redemption.

Memorizing Romans 8:1 provides an excellent escape from the guilt. Repeating this short verse reminds us and our adversary repentance places us above reproach. Christ's blood cleanses, so that even in the midst of discovering we tripped up again, we have the assurance we cannot be condemned because we're in Christ Jesus!

The First Thursday of Lent

*For the law of the Spirit of life has set us free
from the law of sin and death.*
Romans 8:2

Freedom. Everyone longs for it. Yet even in a country where freedom is paramount, people still find themselves in shackles. Bound by worry and anger, confined in fear and doubt. Self-imposed rules and unrealistic standards hold us back. But that's not the life Christ came to give.

I grew up in the perfect family. Unfortunately, perfection requires a lot of regulations and little freedom, and most of my bondage came from what I imagined was expected from me causing a lot of stress.

People look for freedom in money and jobs. Yet those things which boast the most freedom often become the source of our chains. I remember my list of "if onlys". If only I had more money. If only I could meet people's expectations. If only I lived closer to home. The great deceiver had convinced me I could control the monster that squashed my dreams and stole my peace.

Gradually God unveiled an amazing truth. Only Christ can set me free. Jesus poured His grace on me the moment I was ready to receive it. Although nothing in my life changed, when I allowed His Spirit to be in control, the burdens this world asked me to carry became lighter.

In the retrospect and self-examination of Lent lies an opportunity to be set free. When we refuse the condemnation of the enemy and the world and accept instead the life-giving love of Jesus, we find ourselves free from the rules and able to live in the peace the Spirit came to give.

The First Friday of Lent

*What the law was powerless to do,
because it was weakened by the flesh,
God did by sending his own Son
in the flesh to be a sin offering
and so He condemned sin in the flesh.*
Romans 8:3

Humans render the law powerless, and I'm living proof. I relate to the few verses leading into Romans 8. Paul said, "The things I want to do, I do not do. But what I hate, I do." The apostle's frustration resonates. Why then, did God give His people these commandments He knew they could never follow?

Perhaps because He knows His creation better than we know ourselves.

Handcrafted in the image of God, it can be easy to start to believe we are God. Independence creeps in, and our "do it myself" mode creates the illusion we can save ourselves. The law proved otherwise. James tells us whoever fails at breaking one point of the law, breaks all of it.

Our weak flesh makes achieving holiness on our own impossible. God gave the law so we'd see it. He sent Jesus to fix it. On that first Good Friday, Jesus became the offering holiness required. His sacrifice condemned our sin, and separated us from it, so we could live free from sin's condemnation. Lent reminds us of this great act of grace.

Jesus died in my place. Christ rescued my weak flesh and paved the way for me to be reunited with my Father. And He did it for you too!

The First Saturday of Lent

So the righteous requirements of the law
might be fulfilled in us
who do not walk according to the flesh,
but according to the Spirit.
Romans 8:4

Yesterday we recognized the law always had the power to help me be righteous, but my human nature caused it to be weak. That's why Jesus said He didn't come to abolish the law but fulfill it. (Matthew 5:17) He took everything that weakened the perfect law of God, the entire burden of the world's sin, upon Himself. When He died, all our sin died with Him. Those who walk in His Spirit are made righteous because of His death, we now meet the requirements of the book of Leviticus.

I remember my days of walking in the flesh. I wanted to live a good life, but I failed at every turn. Creating a perfect façade became my goal, but eventually the show became too difficult. After I truly surrendered to Christ, I gradually began to let the Spirit lead. In the Spirit the thing that had been hard work came natural.

Good Friday accomplished more than our minds can imagine. Jesus did more than just die in our place; He allowed the sins of the entire world to be placed upon Him like the scapegoat we read about in Leviticus 16. The Messiah became the ultimate sin offering. His sacrifice put an end to the daily offerings Moses prescribed. His death fulfilled the requirements so we can now walk in His Spirit and come confidently into the presence of God.

The First Sunday of Lent

> *¹ Therefore, there is now no condemnation for those who are in Christ Jesus, ² because through Christ Jesus the law of the Spirit who gives life has set you free from the law of sin and death. ³ For what the law was powerless to do because it was weakened by the flesh, God did by sending his own Son in the likeness of sinful flesh to be a sin offering. And so he condemned sin in the flesh, in order that the righteous requirement of the law might be fully met in us, who do not live according to the flesh but according to the Spirit.*
> *Romans 8:1-4*

The early church didn't count Sundays in the forty days of Lent. Instead, they used the first day of each week as a day of celebration. So, let's celebrate!

I celebrate because I am not condemned!

I celebrate because I am free from the law of sin and death!

I celebrate because Christ came to earth and walked in the flesh so I know He understands!

I celebrate because Christ's sacrifice fulfilled the requirements of the law!

Take some time today to celebrate all the beauty Easter and Good Friday bring to our lives. Praise Jesus for condemning sin and saving us!

The First Monday of Lent

Those who walk according to the flesh,
have their minds set on the things of the flesh,
but those who live according to the Spirit
have their mind set on the things of the Spirit.
Romans 8:5

Where is your mind set? That's a question every Christian needs to consider often, perhaps daily. Life litters our path with distractions. Frustration lurks at every turn. Anger hides in the shadows, and judgment lingers even though we feel certain we banished it to the netherworld. So much threatens to move our mindset from the things of the Spirit to the things of the flesh without warning.

I'm amazed at how quickly I lose focus. In the middle of my prayers fleshly thoughts creep in and steal my mindset. As I read scripture, plans for the day ahead divert my concentration, and I have no idea what I just read.

Just another reason I praise God for promising no condemnation for those in Christ Jesus! The Almighty knows our minds will wander. He understands circumstances influence our thoughts.

Unfortunately, we humans try to control our mindset rather than our walk. We beat ourselves up when we daydream during the sermon or fall asleep during our prayers.

Instead we should praise God we made it to worship or remembered to pray. Each time we walk with our Creator and allow His Spirit to live in us, He'll turn our attention back to the One who offered Himself on our behalf and loves us more than we can imagine.

The First Tuesday of Lent

*The mindset of the flesh is death,
but the mindset of the Spirit is peace.*
Romans 8:6

Where is your mind set? Yep, we started with that question yesterday, too. But God must want us to give it some consideration, because you'll find the subject in tomorrow's verse too. I think it's because your mindset creates your perspective, and perspective builds the lens with which we see everything else.

Take my mother for instance. She never made it to five foot tall. Her boss at the local tractor place, on the other hand, stretched over six feet. One day after she set up a display of ball caps, he expressed disappointment because he expected her to put the hats on a shelf at eye level. Imagine his surprise when she confidently told him she had! It's all a matter of perspective.

When your mind focuses on the things of this world, everything gets depressing pretty fast. However, when we look through the lens of the Spirit, we find hope and peace.

Lent makes for a great time to shift perspective. Many folks fast during these six weeks. But rather than food, perhaps our fast should be from negativity. Maybe we need to give up the nightly news or social media.

You still have forty days to walk a bit closer to Christ. You might try a fast or more scripture. Maybe you just need to praise Him more each day. Whatever we do to follow Jesus more closely, we'll discover we begin to look at things through the eyes of the Holy Spirit. The new perspective will offer peace and make a difference in our lives we'll never want to give up.

The Second Wednesday of Lent

*The mindset of the flesh is hostile toward God
because it will not submit to God's law,
nor can it*
Romans 8:7

When we focus on the things of this world, we cannot submit to God. Let that roll around in your brain for a moment.

None of us likes to think ourselves hostile toward God. We follow the Commandments and treat others well. But Paul tells us until we invite the Spirit in, the flesh has control. And with the flesh in charge, hostility toward God reigns.

I grew up a rule follower. For many years I thought my behavior and the legacy of my grandparents gave me an inside track to Christianity. Discovering my good works did nothing to mend my relationship with the Creator was crushing.

The problem lies in those first four commandments. Most humans will agree the final six make life civil. But the Creator said, "No other gods except me." Nothing can come before Him, not our kids or our spouse, not friends or siblings, not our jobs or finances. And how often do we keep the Sabbath holy?

I know . . . we try . . . we mean well. I get it! What will it take for us to stop our feeble attempts and turn our lives over to the Spirit? Lent sets aside forty days to bring a magnifying glass to the party. It gives us an opportunity to examine our hearts and minds and make certain they are set on our Savior.

The Second Thursday of Lent

*Those who walk according to the flesh
cannot please God.*
Romans 8:8

Futility. Most of the world walks in futility. Many talk about God; they hope good works earn brownie points. But few believe they need to make a commitment to the Savior. Thinking it's enough to believe God exists, they ignore James' warning, "you believe that there is one God. Good! Even the demons believe that—and shudder." (James 2:19

Jesus' brother knew firsthand, head knowledge cannot compare to heartfelt faith.

Many acknowledge God created everything and understand Christian history, yet still live in hostility toward Jesus. Romans 10 tells us in order to be saved we must believe deep in our soul that Christ died on our behalf and rose from the dead. Paul reminds us until we make Jesus our Master, we walk in the flesh.

Early in my life I believed following the rules made God happy. I read Romans more than once before discovering none of my goodness brought joy to the Savior.

If you want to please your Creator, "walk with me" leads His short wish list. To commemorate Good Friday and Easter in a way that delights your Heavenly Father, give yourself completely to the One who sacrificed Himself so we could know the fullness of the Holy Spirit.

The Second Friday of Lent

But you do not walk according to the flesh,
but according to the Spirit,
if indeed the Spirit of Christ lives in you.
And anyone who doesn't have
the Spirit of Christ,
does not belong to Christ.
Romans 8:9

Paul graciously assumes his readers walk with Christ, and he's clear, only those who allow the Spirit of Christ to live in them belong to Christ. The entire book of Romans offers the clearest message of salvation. So as a reminder to those who've walked the Romans road, I'll share so you can help others walk in the Spirit. And for those who've not journeyed with Jesus yet, today could be the perfect day!

STEP 1: Realize we can't please God on our own. Sin separated Adam and Eve from God, and it's still keeping humans from their Creator.

Romans 3:23 – for all have sinned and fall
short of the glory of God

STEP 2: Recognize sin and understand that the only thing we earn when from sin is eternal separation from God. Salvation is a gift from Jesus, but we have to accept it.

*Romans 6:23 – The wages of sin is death,
but the gift of God is eternal life.*

STEP 3: Receive God's love. We don't have to be good enough for God, He loves us in spite of ourselves. In fact, He loves us so much, He allowed Christ to take our place on the cross even though He knew some might not even appreciate it.

*Romans 5:8 –
God demonstrated His love for us in this:
While we were still sinners, Christ died for us.*

STEP 4: Rejoice as you pray. There's no special prayer, but we usually begin by acknowledging our understanding of those first three steps. Then we tell Jesus He's our Lord, He's in control! We express our belief in His resurrection and praise Him for His sacrifice on the cross.

*Romans 10:10 & 13 - [10] For it is with your
heart that you believe and are justified, and it
is with your mouth that you profess your faith
and are saved. [13] for, "Everyone who calls on
the name of the Lord will be saved."*

STEP 5: Tell someone. Don't keep your faith to yourself. Find someone to help you grow in Christ.

*Romans 10:9 - If you declare with your mouth,
"Jesus is Lord," and believe in your heart
that God raised him from the dead,
you will be saved.*

The Second Saturday of Lent

If the Spirit of Christ lives in you,
then even though your body
is subject to death because of sin,
the Spirit gives life because of righteousness.
Romans 8:10

We grieve when our loved ones die. No one is exempted. However, Paul reminds us that even though every body will cease to breathe, those who walk with the Spirit of Christ will continue to live because of the righteousness poured out on us through Christ's sacrifice.

I used to fret over verses like this one. What if my prayers didn't matter because "The prayers of the righteous are powerful and effective"? (James 5:16) I knew even on my best day I couldn't achieve righteousness.

Although we have no righteousness of our own, Christ's Spirit grants us His righteousness. At least half a dozen times the Bible tells us righteousness is a gift we can't earn. And with that righteousness comes life from the Holy Spirit.

We will mourn when those we love quit breathing. However, it may help to remember when a person dies in Christ, he passes from this life to the next life without skipping a beat. We will miss them, but our sadness should be mixed with celebration.

Likewise those of us who walk in the Spirit have no fear in leaving this world. I know. We don't like to think about saying goodbye to those we love. But even though sin may try to kill us, in the Spirit, we never truly die!

The Second Sunday of Lent

*⁵ Those who live according to the flesh
have their minds set on what the flesh desires;
but those who live
in accordance with the Spirit
have their minds set on what the Spirit desires.
⁶ The mind governed by the flesh is death,
but the mind governed
by the Spirit is life and peace.
⁷ The mind governed by the flesh
is hostile to God;
it does not submit to God's law,
nor can it do so.
⁸ Those who are in the realm of the flesh
cannot please God.
⁹ You, however, are not in the realm of the flesh
but are in the realm of the Spirit,
if indeed the Spirit of God lives in you.
And if anyone does not have
the Spirit of Christ,
they do not belong to Christ.
¹⁰ But if Christ is in you, then even though
your body is subject to death because of sin,*

> *the Spirit gives life because of righteousness.*
> Romans 8:5-10 (NIV)

It's celebration day! This Sunday we celebrate because we do not walk according to the flesh. On the day you invited Christ to be your Savior, you were sealed with the Spirit. Even if you began your faith journey Friday or yesterday, the Christ's Spirit lives in you. Everyone's faith starts small and grows; but Jesus is all in the moment you ask Him to be your Savior.

Today we praise Christ because He made His home inside us. We rejoice because when we keep our minds set on Him, not only do we have life, we have peace. We celebrate because we possess the righteousness of Jesus Christ and His Spirit gives us life forever!

The Second Monday of Lent

*If the Spirit of the One
who raised Christ from the dead lives in you,
then the Spirit of the One
who raised Christ from the dead
will also give life to your mortal bodies
by the Spirit who lives in you.*
Romans 8:11

  This season gives us an opportunity to focus on preparing to commemorate the death and resurrection of Jesus Christ. The whole point of this season is to help bring clarity to the reason we call ourselves Christian.

  During the past ten days we've been reminded that the Holy Spirit dwells within the followers of Jesus. Just as Paul's confidence in the Savior's ability to give us life begins to rub off on us, he raises the bar. Not only will our Spirit live; Christ's physical resurrection means our mortal bodies will rise too.

  Paul told the people of Corinth, when the final trumpet sounds, the bodies of the dead in Christ will rise first. Then Jesus' followers with breath in their lungs will follow them to Heaven. It will happen so fast no one will see it. Sci-fi fans will think their friends have vaporized. Or if we've shared the truth about Jesus with them, perhaps they'll finally understand what you meant when you said you'd live with Jesus someday.

There's also another side to this coin. In addition to a resurrected body, I believe our Creator wants us to have real life now. In John 10:10 Jesus said He came so we could have life to the full.

As I've grown closer to the Spirit of the One who raised Christ from the dead, I've found life on this planet has more meaning and abundance. Not an abundance of money or possessions, but Christ has given me peace and joy. He's shown me how to love more completely and given me permission to stop trying to please other humans. The Spirit who lives in me has given life to my mortal body right here where I live.

The Second Tuesday of Lent

> *Therefore brothers and sisters,*
> *we have no obligation*
> *to live according to the flesh,*
> *for those who live*
> *according to the flesh will die.*
> *Romans 8:12 & 13a*

That word obligation tripped me up for a while. One translation said a more literal translation could be debt, but that didn't really clear things up. I finally realized a debt is something I'm compelled to pay. So when I rework this verse, it reads, "we have nothing to compel us to live according to the flesh."

Because I live according to the Spirit, nothing can make me live according to the flesh. Still, I put my toes into the mortal's mud hole more often than I like to admit. But Paul reminds me those mistakes don't control me; my faux pax's have no power. They make me messy, but they can't steal my life.

Too often we believe the lie that our missteps mean we walk in the flesh. Those muddy toes simply identify us as human. Jesus told Peter if he'd already been cleansed, all he needed was a foot washing, and then the Savior took care of that too!

It's only those who wade waist deep into the miry muck of the flesh who get sucked in and die. Those who walk in the Spirit . . . well, that's what we'll talk about tomorrow.

The Third Wednesday of Lent

*But if by the Spirit
we put to death
the misdeeds of the flesh
we will live.
Romans 8:13b*

Death is scary. On fear.net dying made it to number eleven on their list of top 100 fears. With the Bible's promise of living forever, you'd think more people would at least give Christianity a try.

After folks accept Christ, one of their greatest fears becomes messing up. I can't count the number of times I've heard people worry about their tendency to sin. Some don't want to let God down. Others fear they'll be subject to death because they walk in the flesh.

But did you see who Paul holds responsible for the crushing the misdeeds of the flesh? We aren't alone. God expects the Spirit to take the lead as we exterminate the misdeeds of the flesh.

How many times have we attempted to get rid of sin ourselves? Oh, we know Christ promised His blood would atone for it. We may even believe His Spirit could kill it. Still we think we can conquer our misdeeds on our own, and we beat ourselves up when we don't change fast enough.

How might things be different if we let the Spirit make the changes? When we accept Christ's sacrifice as the payment for our sins and give the Spirit permission to take care of the residual misdeeds, we're on the right track. Listening to the Spirit will lead us to a place of peace and joy and most of all, life.

The Third Thursday of Lent

Those who walk according the Spirit
are children of God
Romans 8:14

Have you heard the saying "We're all God's children"? Romans 8:14 challenges that statement. Consider Pinocchio. Geppetto created a puppet and wanted to claim him as his son, but adoption was impossible until the wooden marionette became a real boy.

It makes people feel good to call themselves children of God; however, Paul reminds us only those who walk according to the Spirit have a true right to the title. Those who refuse the Spirit of Christ remain puppets, creations of God, but not children of God. If we liken the enemy to the coachman in Pinocchio's story, we see how a puppet can get into trouble when the carver no longer controls the strings.

I remember when I let the world and the enemy control the marionette crossbars. Hoping to make everyone around me happy, I lived the definition of co-dependent. Then I discovered the freedom of becoming a true child of the Heavenly Father. No strings attached, sometimes I still miss my Savior's instructions, but when I walk with Him, I live in His blessing.

As we examine ourselves during these six weeks of preparation, it's good to make certain we walk according to the Spirit. Take a look at where you've traveled and make sure your footprints never linger too long on the path of the flesh. We all meander there from time to time, but children of the King run back as soon as they realize they let go of their Father's hand.

The Third Friday of Lent

*For you did not receive
a spirit of slavery to return to fear
You were given a Spirit of adoption
so you can cry out "Abba, Father."*
Romans 8:15

Do you live as a slave or a son? Jesus poured out His Holy Spirit so we could be free, to keep us from fear. Why then, do so many view Christianity as a cage or prison?

The moment I gave up the puppet strings and allowed myself to become a real girl, God signed my adoption papers. I now call the Master Craftsman, "Papa." I follow His laws, not because I'm a slave with restrictions, but because I'm now His child, and those rules are boundaries to protect me.

Calling God Daddy, Papa or anything else intimate and endearing may seem odd, even disrespectful; but when we embrace the reality of what our adoption means, the truth will not only set us free, but give us an overwhelming sense of just how much Abba loves.

The Third Saturday of Lent

*The Spirit within us testifies with our spirits
that we are God's children.*
Romans 8:16

Have you ever wondered how you can be sure of your salvation? This verse shares the secret. Christ's Spirit confirms it within you.

In my early days of walking in the Spirit, I learned to question my standing in Christ. I worried I might lose my place in the Kingdom and sometimes second guessed my salvation. When I first heard folks express assurance in their relationship with Jesus, I thought they were talking heresy.

But Christ wants us to know we are saved. He puts His Spirit inside of us to confirm the fact!

We can never become too confident in our salvation. Danger comes when we begin to think we can save ourselves. When we count on our own goodness, then we have a problem. But being too confident in our salvation resembles being too confident that the woman who raised you is your mother!

When we walk in the Spirit, we'll begin to hear Him speak to our hearts. It may take time to recognize His voice, but when we do, the testimony He brings will assure us we are God's children.

The Third Sunday of Lent

*[11] And if the Spirit of him who raised Jesus
from the dead is living in you,
he who raised Christ from the dead
will also give life to your mortal bodies
because of his Spirit who lives in you.
[12] Therefore, brothers and sisters,
we have an obligation—
but it is not to the flesh, to live according to it.
[13] For if you live according to the flesh, you will
die; but if by the Spirit you put to death the
misdeeds of the body, you will live.
[14] For those who are led by the Spirit of God
are the children of God.
[15] The Spirit you received
does not make you slaves,
so that you live in fear again;
rather, the Spirit you received
brought about your adoption to sonship.
And by him we cry, "Abba, Father."
[16] The Spirit himself testifies with our spirit
that we are God's children.
Romans 8:11-16 (NIV)*

Happy Celebration Day! The early church leaders didn't include Sundays as part of the 40 days of Lent because they considered each a day of celebration. But these six Sundays didn't hold exclusive rights to the party. All fifty-two Sundays received the designation. Christ defeated death on the first day of the week. Paul called it the Lord's Day. So in antiquity Sundays became set apart.

What about you? Do your Sundays resemble a festival or a fiasco? Few observe Sabbath anymore. I don't mean sitting around bored. I mean making the first day of the week different than the other six. God asked us to make it holy or set apart.

I encourage you to create a new habit during Lent. Retrain yourself and your family to treat Sunday like a jubilee. Feel free to be active; however, let your activity be something you love, something you praise God for.

Abba longs to see you living in joy. He enjoys you and waits for you to join His party. I pray these six weeks will just be the beginning of a year of weekly celebrations.

The Third Monday of Lent

*And if we are children, then we are heirs
-heirs of God and co-heirs with Christ-
and if we share in His sufferings,
then we will also share in His glory*
Romans 8:17

I love my parents, but I'm not counting on their wills to make me rich. My siblings and I will inherit everything, and while it's giving them a comfortable life, I'm happy to say they're using up what might be my inheritance.

On the other hand, my Heavenly Father owns everything. Even the comfort my parents now enjoy belongs to Him. And from the glimpse of Heaven I find in scripture, the beauty of this part of His Creation can't compare to the magnificence of the place He's prepared for me in the future.

Our true inheritance lies in Heaven. There we'll find more abundance than we can imagine, and we will be entitled to share in Christ's glory. Honestly, the thought is beyond my imagination. My human brain can't fully grasp what it means to get any of Christ's glory.

Yet that's what Paul tells us. We will inherit everything our Father owns and share in the riches of Christ, and that includes His glory.

The Third Tuesday of Lent

I consider my present sufferings
not worth comparing
to the glory to be revealed in us.
Romans 8:18

Paul lived a life of suffering. Though stoned on a number of occasions and imprisoned even more often, the apostle managed to stay positive in most of his letters. I believe his perspective fueled his attitude.

I don't have it half as rough as Paul. Not one person has tossed a rock at me because of my faith. Yet I still whine. A couple of years ago the doctors diagnosed me with a weird auto-immune disease, I hurt all over. Not once did I compare my suffering to the glory that would one day be revealed in me.

When suffering comes our way, we have a right to vent and complain. Focusing on the negative seems the logical response. On the other hand, we could look at it from Paul's perspective and choose to keep the positive in our sights.

One day God will reveal the glory He placed within us on the day we accepted our adoption. Magnificence rooted in the shared glory of Christ lies within our reach.

Paul understood life on this earth would continually cause pain. Still, the apostle knew all the pain in the world couldn't compare to the glory that was His in Jesus Christ.

The Fourth Wednesday of Lent

All creation waits eagerly with anticipation
the revealing of God's children.
Romans 8:19

The trees know; the flowers believe. Rivers race to find it, and birds sing because they see the possibility. Only the adopted fail to recognize the excitement on the horizon.

I am busy, and even though I stand in awe of the Creator's handiwork, I sometimes get caught up in what I can see instead of living in the anticipation of the promise.

The unveiling of God's children has been scheduled. God put it on the calendar at the beginning of time, but without the familiar day and month markings, the created finds reading it a bit illusive.

I love the picture Paul paints of God's handiwork holding its breath at the prospect of front row seats to the premier of our true glory. It causes me to find excitement in the expectation and makes me appreciate my place in the family!

The Fourth Thursday of Lent

*Creation has existed in futility
and lives in frustration, not out of choice,
but because of the one who subjected it . . .*
Romans 8:20

How can creation's existence be futile? Humans need the oxygen from trees and plants. We depend on water, animals, and gardens to sustain us. And without the sun, we'd freeze or die of malnutrition and Vitamin D deficiency. That sounds pretty important to me.

Don't you hate it when you're held back because of someone else's limitations? Yet Paul leads me to believe the oceans and the stars have untapped potential. Have you ever thought God might be holding the sun and the moon in check?

These heavenly bodies didn't sin. And even though humans have learned to engineer sinful things from vegetation, plants are innocent too.

As magnificent as creation appears, imagine more. Paul tells us the Creator has been subjecting all of it to frustration, but it won't last forever. In the meantime, as I begin to realize the rain and snow have been reigning in their beauty, my reverence grows for all God spoke into existence.

The Fourth Friday of Lent

> *. . . in the hope that creation itself*
> *would one day be delivered*
> *from the bondage of corruption and decay*
> *into the glorious freedom of God's children.*
> Romans 8:21

Most of us know God promised His chosen will one day be freed from these earthly bodies, but had you considered the rest of creation needs delivered as well? The sin of humans not only stifles our freedom, it brings bondage and decay to the rest of the world.

What will the roses look like when they're free to be all they're created to be? How will we contain the songs when birds lose the constraints of a broken world?

Verse seventeen tells us we will inherit the glory of Christ, and on that day the mountains will be free to dance while the breezes play the tune. Will the stars shine brighter, and the Aurora be unleashed on the equator?

Speculation, that's all I have. But in my imagination, I see eagles flying without fear of pesticides and no one doing any poaching. I envision plants growing free without fear of someone abusing the medicinal gift God placed within. Every way in which humans currently corrupt the beauty of creation will be abolished when creation finds deliverance in the glorious freedom of God's children.

The Fourth Saturday of Lent

*We know that all creation has been groaning
as in the pains of labor until now.*
Romans 8:22

A tree at the edge of my drive creaks. My husband says it will have to come down soon. I live the end of a country road, and after dark the sound is eerie. Today's verse reminds me of that tree. It moans because it's been debilitated by the bondage of decay created when Adam and Eve took that first bite.

Coyotes howl with a haunting bay, and volcanoes rumble a warning. The scurrying of mice through the grass signals their fear of predators. Accustomed to nature's cries of discomfort, we don't think about the noises being the direct result of human imposed corruption.

Lent offers a time to reflect on nature's groanings. How many of these cries have I personally caused, even inadvertently?

Historically the church has used these six weeks as a season of repentance, a time to turn and begin again. We can too. Every groan of nature should encourage us to walk in a way that doesn't compound the bondage of corruption, but instead reflects the beauty of Christ who lives in us.

The Fourth Sunday of Lent

*[17] Now if we are children, then we are heirs—
heirs of God and co-heirs with Christ,
if indeed we share in his sufferings
in order that we may also share in his glory.
[18] I consider that our present sufferings
are not worth comparing with the glory
that will be revealed in us.
[19] For the creation waits
in eager expectation
for the children of God to be revealed.
[20] For the creation was subjected to frustration,
not by its own choice,
but by the will of the one who subjected it,
in hope [21] that the creation itself
will be liberated from its bondage to decay
and brought into the freedom and glory
of the children of God.
[22] We know that the whole creation
has been groaning as in the pains of childbirth
right up to the present time.
Romans 8:17-22*

When Moses carried the glory of the Lord, he kept his face covered. He radiated so brightly no one could look at him.

If we knew we would inherit millions of dollars in five years, we'd celebrate. So then, why don't we rejoice knowing we're about to inherit the glory of Jesus Christ?

All of creation knows it will happen, and it expects to cash in on our triumph. In these few minutes you've been reading, everything around you has been dying, one cell at a time, so slowly we don't notice the hour by hour difference. Decay rules.

However, one day the process will be reversed. The New Heaven and New Earth will reveal itself. Already created, they're waiting in the wings for the stage call from the Director. And on that day Creation will stop groaning; trees will rejoice because never again will they be hollow; brooks will sing for they'll never run dry. And those who bear the image of God will finally be clothed with all His glory.

The Fourth Monday of Lent

*Likewise we,
who have the firstfruits of the Spirit,
groan inwardly as we await our adoption,
the redemption of our bodies.*
Romans 8:23

Have you ever waited for the perfect gift? You have confidence your spouse or your parents bought it, but you can't open the present until Christmas or your birthday.

Similarly, our spirits know something better awaits. The Holy Spirit within us confirms it. Sometimes the waiting is painful. Like knowing the gift of your dreams lies under the Christmas Tree, but you can't have it for two weeks, the Spirit within us groans with anticipation and excitement at what lies ahead.

God adopted us; but the adoption must be finalized. A child might live with his adoptive parents for a year or more before the court officially changes his name. And the grand celebration on what many families call 'Gotcha Day' gives us a glimpse into the heavenly party scheduled for the day of our full redemption.

We'll have days of restlessness as we complete our time on Earth, days when we feel as though we don't belong. I've watched older saints. Those days of discontentment with this planet increase as the children of God move closer to 'Gotcha Day.' The Spirit's anxiousness increases as if He can hear the choir warming up for the festivities. But fortunately, the wait will be worth it!

The Fourth Tuesday of Lent

In this hope we were saved;
but hope that is seen is no hope at all.
Who hopes for what they already have?
Romans 8:24

When a child's adoption becomes final, she receives full family rights. Guaranteed a spot in the will, wealthy parents mean she might come into a tidy sum one day. And until she receives it, she can live in the hope of her inheritance.

Much the same way, on the day we were saved, we received the hope of a beautiful eternity. The Bible gives many insights into our heavenly home. Yet like the young adoptee, we don't get to touch what we hope for until a later date.

These weeks of Lent give us time to focus on our hope. It's easy to get comfortable living in this world and forget we've been promised more. Our restlessness in our waiting can cause us to believe we need more earthly things; however nothing satisfies. More stuff will never fill the groanings within us. Only when God fulfills the promise and takes His children into the Kingdom will we see the magnificence and realize it's even more than we'd hoped.

The Fifth Wednesday of Lent

But if we hope in what we do not have,
we wait for it patiently.
Romans 8:25

The world needs hope. But so many people want to see what they hope for, they want to hold it in their hands. Unfortunately, we've all faced disappointment. We become disillusioned with anything we can't see or touch. Trust issues abound. But those who've learned to walk in the Spirit look at things differently.

The moment we accept Christ as our Savior, we experience a glimmer of hope. For many, it's that tiny flicker that drew them to Jesus. Living in despair with nowhere to turn, we discover the origin of that Light. Hope begins when we realize One man died just to make sure we have a place in heaven and loves us regardless of our past.

As we learn to walk in the Light, we develop a sense of trust. Somewhere deep inside we understand Christ has saved us for bigger and better than we can imagine. Inherently we know there's more we cannot see, but we sense it's something worth waiting for.

The Fifth Thursday of Lent

In the same way,
the Spirit helps us in our weakness,
we don't know
what we ought to pray for.
So He intercedes for us with secret groanings.
Romans 8:26

Would you agree with Paul; you don't know what to pray for? If you're like me, most of the time you think you do. We each have a list we know the Almighty can tackle. I always pray for family and friends. With confidence I ask my Heavenly Father to fix their situation, and usually I give Him specific instructions.

But God says His ways and His thoughts are greater and higher than ours. My prayer suggestions reflect human desire and experience. Both limit the scope of my groanings. And when I stop giving God advice and just watch Him work, I'm always astounded.

God understands our limitations, so He gave the Spirit. The Holy Spirit hears our hopes and dreams. He catches our tears and feels our pain. And then, with all the wisdom of the Father, the Spirit of Christ takes our truest petitions to the King. When we do the work of prayer, put in the time, and offer our hearts and minds to Him, the Spirit speaks to the Holy One on our behalf.

The Fifth Friday of Lent

And the One who searches our heart
knows the mind of the Spirit
because the Spirit
intercedes for us according to God's will.
Romans 8:27

Our dearest friends think they know us; however, deep down, we have hidden places in our heart, crevices where we stash hurts and embarrassments. Some things stay concealed so long we forget we put them there, but the Spirit knows.

Our prayers focus on physical ailments and hardship, and sometimes God gives us those miracles. But the Creator's greater concern is our heart. Christ searches our innermost being. He finds those secret longings and ancient scars.

When we truly allow the Spirit of Christ to move within us, He takes our pain to the Father. He reveals the core of our being so the healing can begin. Our labor and grief become the Spirit's outpouring; our joys and celebrations His songs. Our weakness in prayer becomes powerful and effective when the Spirit of Jesus takes over.

The Fifth Saturday of Lent

*Now we know that God
works all things together for the good
of those who love Him
and are called according to His purpose.*
Romans 8:28

Of the more than 1,100 chapters in the Bible, I love Romans 8 the most. And out of 31,000 verses, Romans 8:28 remains my favorite. Paul moves from remarks about our prayer into assuring his readers God always works for their good.

Sometimes God seems silent. We groan inwardly but wonder if our Father hears. Paul reminds me God doesn't move according to my timetable or my plan. He knows what's best for me, and He's working for my good. The Almighty doesn't promise everything will be good, but He guarantees He'll take even the things that look like mistakes and make them work in my best interest.

Romans 8:28 gives me courage to forge ahead. I believe when Paul said all things, he meant even my mistakes. I used to be terrified I'd walk outside of God's will. My fear of failure paralyzed me. Now when I'm unsure of God's yes, I simply make certain my mission is scriptural and my motivation is love for God. Then I can press on, believing even if I've made a mistake, God will turn it into something good.

The Fifth Sunday of Lent

²³ Not only so, but we ourselves,
who have the firstfruits of the Spirit,
groan inwardly
as we wait eagerly for our adoption to sonship,
the redemption of our bodies.
²⁴ For in this hope we were saved.
But hope that is seen is no hope at all.
Who hopes for what they already have?
²⁵ But if we hope for what we do not yet have,
we wait for it patiently.
²⁶ In the same way,
the Spirit helps us in our weakness.
We do not know what we ought to pray for,
but the Spirit himself intercedes for us
through wordless groans.
²⁷ And he who searches our hearts
knows the mind of the Spirit,
because the Spirit intercedes for God's people
in accordance with the will of God.
²⁸ And we know that in all things
God works for the good of those who love him,

who have been called according to his purpose.
Romans 8:23-28 (NIV)

Has our Lenten journey inspired you to celebrate what will be? Do the promises of your glorious Creator make you break out in song?

Unfortunately, instead of rejoicing in anticipation, some get stuck in the groan. Every single living being, perhaps even the rocks and dirt, inherently knows there's more. Without Christ's Spirit and the hope of our adoption, our dream for a better day in a more beautiful place goes unfulfilled.

Before God formed us, He placed within us the desire for perfect fellowship with Him. People search for it in food and drugs. Some think they've found it in relationships and possessions, but when they're stripped away, they realize they've missed the mark.

Today we celebrate because we hope in what we know to be true even though we can't see it. Christ's Spirit takes our deepest and most intimate thoughts and puts them at the Master's feet. Then Jesus takes our desires and our circumstances and in accordance with God's will works them for our good.

The Fifth Monday of Lent

And those He foreknew
He also predestined
to be conformed to the likeness of His Son
so He could be first
among many brothers and sisters.
Romans 8:29

As God looked at the full span of history before He created the earth, He saw you. Prior to the evening and morning of the first day, Christ knew you. His Spirit smiled and said to the Father, "That beautiful creature will look just like your Son."

Folks get caught up in the mechanics of predestination. After all, it would be handy to assume God has our whole life laid out, with mistakes and mishaps built in. But then we read, "Today I set before you life and death . . . now choose life." (Deuteronomy 30:19) God may know our choices ahead of time, but we obviously still have a choice.

We don't have to fully understand the concept to rest secure in the knowledge our Creator planned for us before the plan began. Romans 8:29 reminds us regardless of the circumstances, no birth is an accident. You were designed by the Master Artist, and His blueprint called for a striking resemblance to our big brother.

The Fifth Tuesday of Lent

And those He predestined, He also called.
And those He called, He also justified.
And those He justified, He also glorified.
Romans 8:30

Before time began God foreknew who would and wouldn't come to Him. He could see some had His heart. He saw you had His heart. And those that did, He called them to join Him. Those that answered, He justified. Lent is a celebration of our justification.

Our sin condemns us. There's no way out of the sentence. Judge, jury, the crowd, they all know we're guilty, and the prosecutor dances with delight.

Until the cross.

The cross didn't just take care of our bail, it cleared our name. Christ's sacrifice paid our debt and erased the verdict. The Savior spilled His blood on all the paperwork. He soaked it, making the charges illegible. No one in heaven even remembers the deadly deed because when the angels look, all they see is the glory of Jesus.

The Sixth Wednesday of Lent

*What shall we say then,
if God is for us,
who can be against us.
Romans 8:31*

Everyone should memorize this verse. When opponents try to crush us, our response should be, "God is for us, does it matter they're against us?"

In the previous verses Paul demonstrated the ways God is on our side. He sends the Holy Spirit to intercede for us. He works all things together for our good. Jesus came to make us family. He chose us before the dawn of creation.

All these facts amaze me. I stand in awe when I consider the Maker of the stars has my back. Folks worship celebrities and causes. They trust jobs and money. Yet not one of these things will defend us. Few who sign paychecks know their employees' names.

Jesus is on your side. And if that's not proof enough, just wait until you take in the final verses of Romans. You'll discover Christ wants to be your rescuer even when the whole world comes against you.

The Sixth Thursday of Lent

For God didn't even spare His own son,
but gave Him up as an offering for us.
Why wouldn't He then graciously give us,
with Christ, every good thing.
Romans 8:32

Next Friday we'll commemorate the crucifixion of Jesus. Some use the word celebrate when they talk about the day, but I find it difficult to celebrate the cruel beatings and degradation my Savior faced.

Paul says God gave His Son as an offering. He reminded his Jewish readers Jesus fulfilled the Levitical requirements. But when I allow my mind to play out the scenes of that horrific event, I can only wish they'd treated my precious Lord with as much dignity as the lambs slaughtered for Passover.

These animals' lives ended with a single slice to the neck. Jesus endured painful torment for a full day.

If, in fact, the Master would allow His Son to face that kind of suffering on our behalf, then we can have confidence God is for us. We can know, without a doubt, our Heavenly Father will graciously give us every good thing.

THE SIXTH FRIDAY OF LENT

*Who then brings charges
against God's chosen?
God is the One who justifies.*
Romans 8:33

Paul sends a gentle reminder, God chose you. If He chose you, will He bring charges against you? Seems unlikely. Did you know Satan's name means adversary? The only one accusing you is the devil. Jealous of your relationship with God, he lays blame and guilt on us in an attempt to convince us to give up our chosen position and join his ranks.

Each time our enemy starts to pour on the accusations, we need to remind him God justifies. The blood of Jesus Christ made us righteous.

For centuries before Jesus came, humans tried to be righteous with zero success. Fortunately, our Heavenly Father always had a plan to be our righteousness. He told Isaiah, "I will make you whiter than snow," and He took care of the prophet's unclean lips with nothing in return but a repentant heart.

As Lent winds down, take a moment to praise God for your chosen status. Let's be extremely grateful God dropped the charges against us and gave us justification instead.

The Sixth Saturday of Lent

Who is it that condemns?
Christ died for us
even more, He was raised from the dead
and now sits at the right hand of God
interceding on our behalf.
Romans 8:34

People who see God as wrath-filled and vengeful don't understand the true nature of the Trinity. Yes, He did allow the Israelites to wipe out entire nations in Canaan; however, we discover he waited until the "sins of the Amorites had reached their full measure." (Genesis 15:16)

The Ruler some call unjust allowed those nations to maintain power until they reached the point of no return in their sin. He only brought about their destruction because He knew their hearts could no longer be restored.

Do you recall the promise of our first day together? God doesn't bring charges. I criticize myself, and the enemy feeds my doubts and insecurities, but Christ does not condemn. Our rejection of Christ's gift empowers the accusations of our enemy. To move past the negativity, it's vital we embrace the truth of these verses.

Jesus came to bring justification and redemption. He lived to give Himself up for us and intercede on our behalf.

Palm Sunday

²⁹ For those God foreknew he also predestined
to be conformed to the image of his Son,
that he might be the firstborn
among many brothers and sisters.
³⁰ And those he predestined, he also called;
those he called, he also justified;
those he justified, he also glorified.
³¹ What, then,
shall we say in response to these things?
If God is for us, who can be against us?
³² He who did not spare his own Son,
but gave him up for us all—
how will he not also, along with him,
graciously give us all things?
³³ Who will bring any charge
against those whom God has chosen?
It is God who justifies.
³⁴ Who then is the one who condemns?
Christ Jesus who died -
more than that, who was raised to life
- is at the right hand of God

and is also interceding for us.
Romans 8:29-34

If we ranked our Sundays according to their potential for celebration, this one deserves to be in the top 10. That Sunday afternoon when Jesus made His way into Jerusalem screamed celebration. Cloaks on the ground mimic our modern day red carpets, and all the branches waving alongside the road from Bethany to Jerusalem resembled a small town parade.

We know from Zacchaeus' story, folks often lined the streets when Jesus came to town, and when He journeyed to Jairus' house to heal his daughter, the crowds were so large they pressed in against Him. But on this day, the people ran ahead and behind Him yelling their praises. I imagine the Savior riding the donkey, the crowds leaving enough space to give the impression of a celebrity riding through.

The verses from Romans we read this week give us cause to celebrate. God does not bring charges. Christ does not condemn. Before time began Jesus knew we would choose Him, so He called and justified. And because Paul uses the past tense, I believe our Father has already begun the glorification process. So celebrate today! Hosanna! Blessed is He who comes in the Name of the Lord!

Holy Monday

*Who can separate us
from the love of Jesus Christ?
Can trouble, hardship or persecution, famine,
nakedness, danger or sword?*
Romans 8:35

This world steals. Every day it robs people of joy and peace. Material loss compounds emotional wreckage. No one is immune from the potential to be left destitute.

Life with Jesus offers something no one can take away. Trouble, hardship, persecution may threaten or attack, yet those who live secure in the love of Jesus know they still have their most valuable possession. Our enemies may leave us without food or clothing, we might have to dodge danger or run from those who want to kill us; however, even when we hide ourselves away for protection, the love of Christ remains with us.

This week is our reminder of the magnitude of that love. Our Savior walked right through His enemy's front door. He invited their torment. Why? Because He loved you. He cherishes you with a love that can never be broken or stolen. Nothing can separate you from His great agape love.

Holy Tuesday

> *As it is written,*
> *"For Your sake we face death all day long,*
> *We are like sheep being led to the slaughter."*
> Romans 8:36

King David faced death for the sake of Yahweh. Saul wanted him exterminated. David's anointing, and therefore, his existence, threatened King Saul's throne and his family's future. Little did the Psalmist know Christ followers would face a similar fate thousands of years later.

I feel blessed. The worst I face is mocking or being shunned. Our brothers and sisters in other countries don't enjoy the same freedoms. They can relate to this quote from Psalm 44.

As we move closer to the main event of the season, may we praise Christ for our ability to worship unhindered. Let's take time this week to pray for those who risk persecution when they meet or witness. And I pray we never take for granted our freedom to gather.

Holy Wednesday

*But we are more than conquerors
through the One who loves us.*
Romans 8:37

Do you feel like a victor? Most don't. Too often pickle jars and simple gadgets win the battle, and the bigger trials of life can be overwhelming. If someone introduced us as a conqueror we'd laugh.

Yet because Jesus Christ loves us, and we've chosen to live "in Christ," Paul calls us conquerors. Our Savior won the battle against death, hell, and the grave through the cross and resurrection. We've spent forty days preparing to celebrate this victory.

But how often do you put Christ's victory in your win column? Though we commemorate Christ's death and resurrection every year, we forget His triumph is our triumph, too.

And even more exciting, our decision to follow Christ seals the deal on the enemy's defeat. He works to stop us and give us grief. But as we determined on Holy Monday, though he tries with all his might, he can't separate us from our Savior's love. Because of our Redeemer, we have more than conquered.

Holy Thursday

For I am convinced that neither death nor life,
angels nor demons,
things in the present nor the future,
nor any powers
Romans 8:38

Those in Christ Jesus have certain assurances. Paul was completely convinced that whether he lived or died, He was in Christ's love. Angel worship might tempt him, and demons could torment, still Yahweh loved him. Not even his past persecution of Christians could keep Jesus from loving him.

Today is Maundy Thursday, the anniversary of the day Jesus celebrated His Last Supper with the inner circle. We call it Maundy because Christ gave His mandate, His new command, "Love one another as I have loved you."

It was a grave night for the disciples. Jesus told them things they didn't really want to hear. The mood in the room may not have been as light as in years past. Jesus may have been a little pensive knowing His torment and crucifixion lay only hours ahead.

The followers of Christ didn't know what we know, death isn't big enough to hold back the love of our Lord Jesus Christ.

Good Friday

Not height or depth,
nor anything in all creation
can separate us from the Love of God
which is in Christ Jesus.
Romans 8:39

The eleven thought it was over. Paralyzed by fear, only John followed Christ to the cross. Jesus was being taken away, and they believed this separation from their Friend and His love would last forever.

The apostles didn't know what you and I know. Paul hadn't yet written this verse, and the truth in it lay out of their reach.

Satan stood on the victors' podium for a few hours as the Pharisees and Sadducees reveled in their win. Confident they controlled the fate of the Nazarene, how could they know the One they'd killed had orchestrated every step to demonstrate the powerlessness of life, death, rulers, heights, depths and creation.

Good Friday empirically proves the depth of the Father's love. We see the enormous lengths Jesus will go because of His affection for us. Nothing in all creation could have kept Him from hanging on the cross, because nothing in all creation could stop Him from showing you how much He loves.

Holy Saturday

*³⁵ Who shall separate us
from the love of Christ?
Shall trouble or hardship
or persecution or famine
or nakedness or danger or sword?
³⁶ As it is written:
"For your sake we face death all day long;
we are considered as sheep to be slaughtered."
³⁷ No, in all these things
we are more than conquerors
through him who loved us.
³⁸ For I am convinced
that neither death nor life,
neither angels nor demons,
neither the present nor the future,
nor any powers,
³⁹ neither height nor depth,
nor anything else in all creation,
will be able to separate us
from the love of God that is in
Christ Jesus our Lord.
Romans 8:35-39*

The day after Christ's death is a day of silence in scripture, and I'm sure the silence was deafening in a small corner of Jerusalem that day. The disciples didn't feel like conquerors. Hardship and persecution had drained them. As far as they were concerned it was over. The cross had crushed every dream and plan. Death had separated them from the One person who had finally shown them the true meaning of love. Confused and alone, even though they were probably all together, the eleven and the women who had followed Mary and Joseph's son were devastated and lost.

When we forget the truth of Romans 8, we too become confused and lost. Sometimes the world hijacks us. We get thrown off course and forget that nothing can separate us from Christ's love. These final verses may be the most important for us to understand. When trouble and hardship, danger and persecution strike, we can remind the enemy that nothing, absolutely nothing in all of creation can keep Christ, along with His Spirit and His Father from loving us with a love that is bigger than we can possibly imagine.

Easter

Therefore, there is now no condemnation
for those who are in Christ Jesus

. . .

If God is for us, who can be against us.
He who did not spare His own Son,
but gave Himself up for us all

. . .

Christ Jesus who died
more than that, was raised to life
sits at the right hand of God interceding for us.

. . .

In all these things we are more than conquerors
through Him who loves us.
From Romans 8

Each Sunday we've been celebrating. Today we've reached the moment of ultimate celebration. The day originally set aside for worship moved from Saturday to Sunday because of the resurrection. Early followers knew this event marked a turning point in the faith.

Because of the resurrection, I am no longer condemned. My Father held nothing back. He sacrificed His precious Son for my sake.

Easter reminds us we follow a mighty King. He won the ultimate battle when He defeated death, and He passes along the power of the resurrection to those devoted to Him. But what do we do with the authority God gives us?

In the midst of this holy celebration, it's easier to believe we're more than conquerors, but what about tomorrow? When hospital bills pour in or your health deteriorates, will you cling to the victory of the resurrection? When friends and family may desert you, will you remember you can never be separated from the love of Jesus.

This is the promise of Easter. It's the culmination of every prophecy as well as tremendous evidence of the love and power of Jesus Christ. The celebration of the resurrection shouldn't be limited to one day. This party should go on for the rest of the year. As we embrace the truth of this gift, our faith will grow, the Spirit will have more room to work, and we will truly become more than conquerors in the love of Jesus Christ.

Thank You

Thanks so much for journeying through Lent with me. If you've enjoyed these devotions, I'd truly appreciate a review on Amazon or my website. In addition, I invite you to join me during Advent.

On the following pages you'll see a few more resources I've created. I love sharing my aha moments and the things Christ has revealed. I hope some of them can be a blessing for you too!

More Resources by Lynne

RESOURCES FOR ADVENT
Advent Through the Eyes of Mary
Leave the Empty Boxes Behind
Journey to Bethlehem
The Angels Speak
A Christmas of Heavenly Peace

RESOURCES FOR YOUR CHILDREN'S MINISTRY
Journey to Greatness
Jesus, Teach Me How to Pray
Heroes, Heroines, Champs and Chumps
The Fruit of the Spirit is . . .
Children of the King

BIBLE STUDY DISCUSSION GUIDES
Dive In to a Life of Freedom
Bible Studies to Give You Hope
Running the Race
A Future and a Hope

Visit www.LynneModranski.com
to see these resources and more

Devotions for Church Leaders and Small Groups

Leaders growing in the likeness of the Almighty are essential to the body of Christ, as are fellowship groups. These seventy-five short meditations were written with these important people in mind. Each uses scripture to help leaders focus on Christ. In addition to inspiring followers of Jesus, each message can easily be a sermon starter or springboard for discussion.

Devotions Inspired by Life

Buzzards, blue jays, ice cream and snowflakes. What do have in common? Each one can teach us something about Jesus! Jesus constantly used illustrations from everyday life to teach His disciples. He shared countless parables. In the same way God blesses us daily with aha moments. He uses simple things in creation to reveal Himself. When we learn to see the Almighty work in everything, we can grow in Christ and find more joy in the journey.

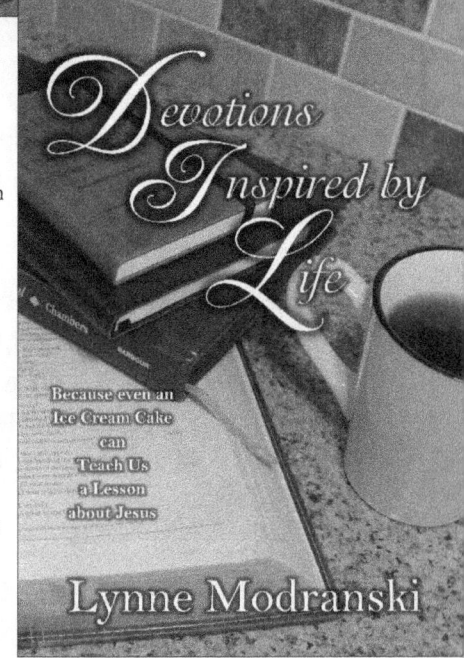

www.ingramcontent.com/pod-product-compliance
Lightning Source LLC
Chambersburg PA
CBHW031409040426
42444CB00005B/480